# THE FOURTH REFLECTION

*Catching glimpses of the future from*
*the hilltops of the past*

I0638626

# THE FOURTH REFLECTION

*Catching glimpses of the future from the hilltops of the past*

Wayne Allen LeVine

THOMAS NOBLE BOOKS

Thomas Noble Books

Wilmington, DE

www.thomasnoblebooks.com

ISBN: 978-1-945586-01-9

Library of Congress Control Number: 2016912024

Printed in the United States of America

First Printing: 2016

Editing by Gwen Hoffnagle

# DEDICATION

This is to wonder, inspiration, and the edification of everyday life. This is to adventure, discovery, and the courage to create. This is to openness, eagerness, and unbridled expression; to passion, love, and empowering friendship. This is to the ebb and flow of human emotion; to clarifying thought and decisive action. This is to my mother and father, Margaret and Jack . . . for the gift of life they granted me, and the riches of gratitude they helped foster. This, most of all, is to my wife, soul mate and true best friend Robie and our two gifted sons Ryan and Justin -- who have raised their loving parents well by teaching us the momentous moment by moment meaning of life!

# CONTENTS

# INTRODUCTION

*The Fourth Reflection* is really a dance — a thought-provoking tango between the romance of the present and the prevalent enchantment of the past. It's about chance and circumstance, rebellion and redemption, adventure and discovery, experimentation, revelation, and chaos and it's illuminating opposite. It's about making calculated leaps and attempting more than a handful of seemingly foolhardy hurdles — a beneficent tome intent not only on pushing the envelope but setting it on fire and mirthfully scattering its proverbial ashes across the balmy, sun-drenched, wind-swept landscape of the collectively creative unconscious — a tantalizing first-person confession that could be used as a kind of linguistic ballast for this crazy/beautiful ship we all find ourselves in.

This is a book about breaking rules, shaping perspectives, and running red lights, metaphorically speaking. It's about being naked in public — soulfully exposed for the sake of starting from the heart of what really matters. Vulnerability is essential to being our absolute best — one of the magical keys for unlocking our courage and strength and claiming them as our own, because they are! It explores some of the many possible benefits of doubt while unwrapping and exposing the true gifts of solitude.

Forward, then back and forth again — that's really how this book was written, which is the meter and measure of how many, if not most of us, tend to live our lives, although I lack the audacity to speak with authority on anyone's life aside from my own. *The Fourth Reflection* was written in alignment with the rhythm of my life, in sync with my own heartbeat. This I can say with a deep sense of certainty. Missing a beat from time to time is an inevitable part of any truly impassioned, fully lived life. Retrospection is part of that rhythm as well. Those deep, bold, indelible impressions continue to bring our faithful recollections to life whenever and wherever we opt to employ them. Memories are more than merely imaginative portals to our evaporative past; they are invaluable parts of our true here-and-now, and need not be sacrificed upon the illusory altar of "what has passed is past."

If I've learned anything at all along the way, it's that life is cyclical — a perpetually back-and-forth, here-again there-again, ever-unfolding, intermittently challenging, wild, and wondrously rhythmical ride through the sentient fullness of life. And I've learned that sharing the ride of my life with creatively driven people like you adds depth and dimension to my own everyday while shining an exquisite light on the extraordinary meaning and purpose of being *alive*!

# CHAPTER 1

---

# The Gifts of Travel

# Somewhere Out There

It was the perfect time for travel, exploration, and real-world discovery. Adventure beckoned — and I was unencumbered enough to listen and respond. It was more than merely the call of the wild; it was the call of culture as well. I yearned for landscapes I had yet to step foot upon.

*"It's a dangerous business, Frodo, going out your door.*
*You step onto the road, and if you don't keep your feet, there's no*
*knowing where you might be swept off to."*
— *Bilbo Baggins in J. R. R. Tolkien's The Lord of the Rings*

I longed for sights and sounds that were far and away from my Windy City hometown. I wanted to taste cuisine that could only be found in countries a considerable distance from the borders of my own, and savor art and architecture relished for centuries by scores of men and women much like me in many ways. I wanted to discover ways of conversing with those who don't speak my language, or I theirs. I wanted to dance, drum, and happen upon the many life-enriching wonders that thrive on every continent. I wanted to broaden my horizons, stretch my awareness, widen my perception, and surmount more than merely the geographical limitations of what I felt eager to let in. I wanted to expand my youthful point of view and nurture my soul with the fresh yet ancient scents of human history while mapping the geography of the psyche along the way and charting a path toward a life I felt determined to live fully.

I fancied myself an explorer — a man of the world with a wanting to see, know, and touch directly what books alone can never teach us. Experience is the route that awakens us! Experience — fresh, new, spontaneous involvement in and with the world at hand, in the process of continuous discovery — creates conditions through which healthy, robust, vital synapses can develop and spark new life by virtue of the perfect pairing of two hearty and determined chromosomes.

When "life forever fresh and new" is uniquely experienced and fully embraced, it soaks deeply into our bones and sinews, saturating our psyche with a perpetually unfolding understanding of the miraculous newness of life.

That's what travel offers and allows us. That's what pushes us out our doors and turns us into courageous explorers. We want to see what we have not yet seen, including a better, broader, and more direct view of ourselves. That's what we go in search of — and hope to find "somewhere out there." That's our quest for fire — and it burns within us all the while, no matter what time we're born into, how we are raised, or in what city, country, or village our life journeys begin. It's part of our primal longing, carried in the hub of who we are and wish to become all the more. We are an integral part of the great pulse of life — part of the exquisite mystery we continue to search for in our quests to reveal who we were born to be by living out this life that began with the dream!

> "Life begins with the dream and proceeds outward from there."
> – C. G. Jung

It was time to heed the call of the cultural, historical wild — the ideal time to respond to my innermost summons by honoring that intrinsic invitation to explore and discover more of the world. **Adventure beckoned, and I was eager to align myself with what was calling.** It was time to test the wings of my fledgling philosophy and find out how it and I might soar and glide on Middle Eastern and European currents.

I was immersed, at that time, in my studies of comparative religion, world philosophy, mythology, and Jungian psychology. I was also deeply steeped in my daily practice of Kundalini yoga coupled with years of training and discipline through martial arts. Try fitting all that into a standard-sized backpack and still have room for clothing and shoes. In other words, I was determined to take a whole lot more than a backpack could possibly hold.

I sold my much-loved Volkswagen Sun Beetle, bought a new backpack, purchased a Eurail pass, and booked a flight to the Holy Land via Swiss Air. I left Chicago about three weeks later, departing from O'Hare airport, one of the busiest in the world, and landing on a dirt airstrip on the outskirts of Tel Aviv nearly twenty hours later following a brief stopover in Zurich. I thought I'd begin my journey in the midst of a seemingly endless ancient feud between the "big three" monotheistic faiths of Middle Eastern origin, also known as the Abrahamic religions — Judaism, Christianity, and Islam. I thought I'd start there just to see what I might make of it. And what it might make of me.

I wound up spending four-and-a-half months in the Middle East, long enough to partially process my initial culture shock. Most of my romantic notions about what I thought I might find there were dissolved rather abruptly once I got to what many still refer to as the Holy Land. Whether it is or isn't considered "holy" depends entirely upon us. If we step lightly over the ground beneath our feet, we're more likely to sense what makes it sacred. If we stroll eagerly, albeit respectfully across familiar or unfamiliar land, the inextricable relationship we have with whatever ground we stand on becomes all the more apparent and profound. What makes any land "holy land" rests largely on how we treat ourselves and others — friends, foes, strangers, and loved ones — in relation to our immediate surroundings. How we tread upon the landscape of our eternal soul determines the rhyme and rhythm of our every step.

> *"Intelligence without ambition is a bird without wings."*
> *— Salvador Dali*

# A Handful of Holy Land Highlights

Sleeping beneath those stars in the Sinai for nine or ten nights, watching an array of shooting stars flash across the cosmos each and every night I slept, dreamt, and awakened in the desert.

Swimming through colorful, ancient coral caves intertwined with giant moray eels while snorkeling along those lively reefs lining the shores of the Red Sea.

Moving effortlessly beneath the waves with astonishing schools of phosphorescent fish of every imaginable and unimaginable shade and color darting in and out of my underwater visions.

Seated at a small, round table, sipping tea with milk and honey in a courtyard in Tzfat or Safed, depending upon who you talk to — a city in the north of Israel considered by some as one of the Four Holy Cities in that region of the world. I knew it as Tzfat, as I sat in that courtyard sipping tea and savoring sweet, delectable, purple grapes — dark, shiny grapes that I was invited to pick from spirited vines growing upward along walls of stone that help create the restorative space that defines the sensory threshold one discovers in a courtyard such as that. Tzfat is also known as a long-established artists' colony in the hub of the Holy Land, attracting a wide array of creative souls — painters, sculptors, poets, and scholarly mystics from near and far. I sat drinking tea and conversing with a few of the artists I met in that remarkable courtyard. I sat with strangers who were friends, while remembering friends who seemed like strangers from where I sat.

Those enlivening moments that we're able and willing to fully savor can be tasted for a lifetime. They are the lasting gifts that continue to guide us through the steadily unfolding phases that shape, inform, and inspire our awareness of a fruitful, productive, well-lived life while bearing the weighty darkness of also knowing the juxtaposed existence of its opposite. My delectable recollections of eating freshly baked bread in old Jerusalem, drinking water from a forbidden fountain atop the Mount of Olives, and ducking my head beneath the stony entryway to ancient, unnamed catacombs guided by a middle-aged man with a delightfully reverberant voice telling captivating tales along the way while carrying a fiery torch to light that subterranean path as we sauntered through a history I was permitted to sense, but could never fully know.

After nearly five months of living in the land of milk and honey, I decided it was time to blend some of those sights, sounds, and potent discoveries with a rich array of French, Italian, British, Swedish, Dutch, Norwegian, and many other European impressions yet to be made upon the living clay of my impressionable psyche. I was far from home, and my appetite for travel, adventure, and worldly discovery had barely begun to be appeased. In fact, I was hungrier than ever! I was starving all the more for a deeper sense of who I was and wished to become. Knowing who we are tends to ease the often weighty burden of figuring out what we truly want and need to do. At least we hope that it will — while in the throes of attempting to sort it all out and identify the dream or dreams we're meant to manifest with respect to our own co-created fate and destiny.

*"All we have to decide is what to do with the time given us."*
*– Gandalf in J. R. R. Tolkien's The Lord of The Rings*

We travel to live. And live to travel. And we do both so that we might gain insight through the practice of greeting each hour as part of the marvelous mystery that needn't be solved. When we choose to involve ourselves in any such practice, we're far more likely to take notice of things that would not have been seen had we lacked that exhilarating urge that feeds our eagerness for adventure and discovery. When we attempt to live each day as a perpetually robust *tour de force*, we're bound to fall short of our own expectations at times. But even our shortfalls are likely to leave us a bit higher and hopefully wiser than we were the day before.

# Travel Continued

Socrates said, "The feeling of wonder is the mark of the philosopher, for all philosophy has its origin in wonder."And with that deep sense of wonder in tow, my travels continued. From the Holy Land to the Netherlands — from Rotterdam to Amsterdam — where I fed pigeons in the town square and have pictures to prove it.

Amsterdam, where I relished my heart-warming visit to the Van Gogh museum, feasting upon the largest collection of masterful paintings produced by that beautiful, brilliant, albeit tortured man and artist, Vincent Van Gogh.

Climbing that steep, narrow staircase that leads to the attic Anne Frank and her family secretly lived in for a time, where she penned her world-famous diary in that surprisingly tiny, temporarily safe little space while Holland was under Nazi occupation. It was a heart-wrenching visit that left an indelible impression on the tender underbelly of my soul.

Amsterdam — with its criss-cross canals that line and wind around and through the city, idiomatically referred to as the Venice of the North. A city of copious bridges and a multitude of busy bakeries, with the enticing scents of savory pastries and freshly baked breads wafting through old-city air freshened by northern sea breezes. When one is thriving primarily on the traveler's diet — consisting largely of bread and cheese and/ or cheese and bread — bakeries such as those I discovered in the Netherlands are nothing less than absolute blessings. Dutch breads and pastries — especially while they're still slightly warm, fresh from an earthen womb in the guise of a historic brick oven

— offer both the flavor and the feeling of what our daily bread is meant to be. We are permitted to savor more than the flavor; we are permitted to savor the very essence, the aura, the essential elements of Heaven on Earth, the sprouted ingredients of true aliveness baked into our luscious bread of life! And those cheese shops — typically found in close proximity to those extraordinary bakeries — are as delectable as one might have the good fortune to stumble upon on any continent, anywhere in the world.

**Anywhere in the world...** the last four words of the line above wanted to begin the sentence that followed it. And I complied, in part because real-world stories have a life of their own, and because I intend to stay faithful with all of those spirited details now acting as gills, oxygenating my awareness while allowing me to breathe freely beneath the waters of these lively recollections. These lyrical remembrances have stood the test of time, maintaining their integrity and spirit of innocence by demanding they be told without embellishment. Because life, I'm reminded as I begin to retell them, is not only stranger than fiction, but more exquisite and astonishingly mysterious.

I want to assure you this is leading somewhere — to a point I've yet to make but fully intend to. There is a method to this antithesis to the *non compos mentis* avoidance of life. And therein lies the meaningful retelling of any memorable tale. Every memory is inextricably linked to the lively and intoxicating moment at hand. And when we tap into them — with our full, unfettered presence of mind — nostalgia becomes more than a quixotic gateway to our evaporative pasts. Nostalgia, in that sense, can be used as a kind of omnipresent lens we look through to catch glimpses of the future while standing upon those hilltops of our pasts. Nostalgia, from that perspective, is an enlivening component of our big, bold, perpetually unfolding, and ever-mysterious here-and-now! Those heartfelt recollections help strengthen and lengthen the threads we unravel as we shuffle through the fertile labyrinths of our purposeful lives.

We need to be present, open, and fully attentive to our steadily reawakening pasts. **A written story is a fresh creation of our tethered thoughts and anchored emotions being liberated from their metaphysical mooring posts.** We write them and tell them again and again in order to live them more than once by touching upon the magic that allows us to transcend both the real and imagined limitations of time.

*"Traveler, there is no path,*
*The path is made by walking."*
— *Antonio Machado*

I wanted to be a traveler — a stout-hearted explorer as opposed to a tourist. However, there are touristy things well worth taking in, like the many museums not to be missed. I visited Viking ships in Norway, Denmark, and Sweden. I slept on a ship in Copenhagen that had been turned into an immaculate hotel docked near the Langelinje Pier in close proximity to that world-famous sculpture of *The Little Mermaid* inspired by Hans Christian Anderson's well-known fairy tale.

I spent a significant portion of a perfectly magical day at Frogner Park, also known as Vigelandsparken, in Oslo, Norway, where I was deeply moved and intermittently mesmerized by hundreds of bronze and granite sculptures representing the steadily flowing cycle of human life.

*"I was a sculptor before I was born. There was no other path,*
*and no matter how hard I may have tried to find one,*
*I would have been forced back."*
— *Gustav Vigeland*

Those magnanimously sculpted expressions are the lifelong achievement created by Gustav Vigeland. That old cliché "It's a walk in the park" is bound to take on a whole new meaning if the park you're walking through is, in fact, Frogner Park, in Oslo, Norway.

I so cherished my time there — the park, the people, the lovely late September weather, and the lake I sat near while writing a postcard to my very dear friend Shane, the brother my parents did not give birth to. After feasting on some bread and cheese and quenching my thirst with a sweet, refreshing bottle of sparkling apple cider, I sat on the grass near a murky green lake and wrote this:

My Dear Friend,

At the moment I am sitting under a willow tree in the beautiful Vigeland Park. To my left sits a flock of geese, to my right a flock of seagulls, and directly in front of me floating on the lake are some swans. A minute ago one of the swans came to visit... he walked right out of the water to where I'm sitting, bit my foot, and returned to the water. The birds are amazing, the sculptures are amazing, most of Norway is pretty amazing. I hope you are well and meeting lots of women. You would go crazy over the blondes here!

See you soon,

Wayne

That postcard I wrote and sent way back when found its way back to me a little more than a decade later, after my friend, my brother Shane, passed on. He transitioned on the fourth of July — allowing his spirit to watch the fireworks while ascending. That's a whole other story I won't tell now, or I'll never get to the point I've yet to make. I will say, with loving gratitude, that he was my friend — the brother who clearly enriched my life. He was loved! And still is.

# Birthplace of the Renaissance

All roads may not actually lead to Rome... Florence, Venice, Pisa, or Naples, for that matter. But I was in Europe, and would have been remiss not to visit those cities in the country considered by many to have been the birthplace of the Renaissance and home to many of the most famous and well-loved paintings, sculptures, and refurbished ancient frescos in all the world.

*"Life is nothing but the detours of art seeking to find those one or two images in the face of which our heart first opened."*
*— Albert Camus*

# When in Rome

I found a road that did indeed lead to Rome, and I'm so very glad that I did. When in Rome, whatever else you opt to see and do, visiting the Vatican simply must be among them. It's good to look up and take notice of things beyond the top of one's own head. The ceiling of the Sistine Chapel, arguably the most famous ceiling in the world, is something to look up to and get lost in for a time. Michelangelo began the arduous task of creating that rather revelatory ceiling in July of 1508... alone, reluctant, and relentless. And his imaginative Old Testament frescoed depictions were finally unveiled in October of 1512 — a four-year undertaking that was anything but a steady, unwavering labor of love, having done nearly all he could do to get out of it.

"This is not my true profession," he complained. "I am wasting my time, and all for nothing. May God help me!" That is but one of the anguished expressions found in his letters. It's hard to reconcile the astonishing result of such fierce resistance, making his monumental achievement all the more remarkable, if not miraculous, knowing he was acting against his own will. I stood there in the chapel gazing up at that sensational ceiling covered in colorful biblical tales. I stood there feeling gratefully stirred, though less deeply touched than while taking in the immaculate marble beauty of *The Pieta*.

That ceiling made me think, ponder, muse, and philosophize. The Madonna, on the other hand, provoked pure emotion. Marble made to look so flesh-like I could almost believe there was, in fact, a pulse within that lively creation carved from the finest block of marble ever cut from the quarries of Carrara. I stood there fixed upon the flesh of marble and those folds of cloth that scantly covered it. And that flawless face of the Madonna… exquisite and much younger than anyone other than Michelangelo would dare to imagine. I stood there doing my best to repress my unexpected urge to weep — doing my damnedest to hold back my tears. And I did, but for one that fell slowly for the Agony and Ecstasy of all creation — father and son, God and man, woman and man… woman and child.

I was tempted to step into the Trevi Fountain. But logic got the better of me, and I resisted. I was thousands of miles from home, with a rather limited wardrobe, and no desire to add the weight of soaking-wet clothing to my backpack. I simply peered into that fountain instead, soaking my senses in the sounds of water pouring over sculpted stone and the cleansing waves of children's laughter. I tossed a coin toward the fountain before making my way to the old Spanish Steps. I threw it forward — in my own fashion — facing the fountain so I could see it land. It flew far enough to hit Neptune's right foot, bouncing but a little before falling to the bottom of that famous and beautiful fountain's water basin.

Tradition has it that a traveler will return to Rome if they throw a coin into the ever-flowing waters of that fountain. The coin, however, is to be thrown backward over one's shoulder without looking back. Perhaps there really is something to that old tradition... I threw my coin forward while looking the entire time, and haven't been back there since that day.

I opted not to step into Trevi Fountain, but I did step into the Colosseum — all the way in, with a rather unexpected though understandable sense of eeriness. One does not mosey through the Colosseum — a lighthearted stroll through what remains of it is pretty unimaginable to me. Nonetheless, I continued to move through what was left of that remarkably haunting architectural accomplishment. While stepping slowly around and over those cumbersome circles of brick and stone, I was surprised by an army of shabby cats — scrawny, underfed, homeless felines making their way through those evocative ruins just as I was. I kept moving, walking reverently, with whatever bits of grace I could rally. More cats! Worse off than those I had previously witnessed. Hungry, wounded, scared balls of fur over lingering bones.

Some had missing limbs, some had one eye, and one had been freshly bloodied by a much larger cat prepared for battle, like the ghosts of so many nameless gladiators that seemed to still be trapped there.

# By Way of Gondola

Venice — rising from the shimmering waters of its own dream-like reflections. A city of majesty and wonder built upon water, forever mirroring its own living imagination. Paul McCartney and Wings were playing an open-air concert the night I arrived. I could hear it rather clearly while floating in a gondola on the Grand Canal, en route to my dingy old affordable hotel. And come morning, as the sun ascended above that ancient city, I made my way to Saint Mark's Square.

This was the antithesis of any sense of nostalgia — a territory utterly unknown to my feet and soul, the opposite of déjà vu, wherein everything I could see and sense seemed so resoundingly new! I sat with that awareness, sipping delicious cappuccino while seated shoulder to shoulder with other travelers at a crowded cobblestone-street café. I sat there, in that ancient city, soaking in some of what I had longed to lay eyes on, while eavesdropping on a slew of impassioned conversations… the music of more than a dozen languages in consonance with that sentiently affluent moment at hand.

Those affluent moments, extending the hours that fill in the days that keep us eagerly steeped in discovery, become the indelible stories that carry the meaning we touch, unfold, and continue to realize throughout the twisting, turning courses of our lives.

*"In the winter, Venice is like an abandoned theater.*
*The play is finished, but the echoes remain."*
*— Arbit Blatas*

If this is beginning to sound as if I'm all over the map, I would hope you understand the most obvious reason why... which is, of course, because I am! I may in fact be all over the proverbial map, though fully aligned with the idiomatic nature of this continuous theme that is travel. I may be moving rather quickly from country to country — doing my best to maintain a lively pace without the risk of losing you en route to where this is leading. I have no wish to spread myself thinly or allow my thoughts to become haphazardly scattered along with my lofty recollections of those lands I walked and danced on years ago.

My primary job as writer, narrator, and unofficial travel guide, is, above all else, to earn your trust and hold your interest. If I've failed to do that, then I've done a very poor job, and I do apologize. I pray that's not the case, and that my apology is utterly unnecessary. If you're still with me, I implore you to stay with me, because we're not there yet! We have further to go to get home.

This chapter on travel is not what I intended to write at the outset. I only meant to pen a few highlights — a few choice moments prompted by my travels — and quickly leap to the point; the point I promise to get to a little further down the road. The short story I originally had in mind has somehow morphed itself into a memoir-esque manuscript demanding arresting specificity and an arrangement of evocative details that make a wordy journey worth taking in. I know where this is leading; I've known all along. There is a point I vow to get to. But if I were to blurt it out prematurely in my zealousness to get us there, I would rob us of the journey, which is always the point.

*"When we dance, the journey itself is the point, as when we play music the playing itself is the point."*
*— Alan Watts*

So, dear reader — dear friend, enjoy the music of my indelible memories and these dancing highlights leading the way from page to page. This is nothing more or less than a collection of meaningful moments along the way — a sensual assortment of lively highlights that best describe the travels that have proven instrumental in shaping awareness that continues to enrich and guide my life. Every page thus far has been guided and directed by highlights; by intuitive dreams and imaginings coming to life in the midst of my real-world adventures. Every day is a gift, an offering, an enticing opportunity to give and receive. And if we open up to it — open into it — highlights unfold, come to life, and bless the time we've been given. Now let's get going; we have a train to catch!

# Always Leave Room for Spontaneity

I was on a train from somewhere to somewhere else — I can't really say for certain where I was headed or headed from; we forget where we are at times when we're moving from country to country, city to city, town to town, faster than the speed of our own internal sounds! We need to slow down a bit, rest awhile, and give our psyches time to catch up — so, while on a train from here to there, somewhere to somewhere, while thoroughly steeped in a sleep-deprived haze of dazzling fresh impressions, I had the great good fortune to meet two blonde, blue-eyed American girls eager to exchange travel tales with this blue-eyed American boy.

I don't remember if they mentioned where they were going, but I vividly recall their telling me about more than merely the whereabouts of the place they had just left. "Have you been to Austria?" they asked in exuberant unison. "Are you planning to go?" Actually, I wasn't. "We were in Innsbruck for a week," one of the two glowing girls told me. "We had planned to stay three days, and wound up staying a week. We loved it. It's so beautiful — the Alps are amazing. It's definitely been one of the highlights of our travels so far." "How long have you been traveling?" I asked. They told me they'd been traveling through Europe for more than three months. That surprised me a bit, since they both looked as fresh as mountain snow to me.

Their excitement was contagiously palpable and plausible enough to encourage this traveler to board a train to Innsbruck. I arrived in the middle of the night — a little after 3:00am. The city was asleep when I got in. Nothing was open. A delightful hush seemed to hold that old city in a kind of collective dream — a dream I felt eager to be part of. Even the echoes were respectfully muted; not entirely silent, but softened by the slowness of those ambrosia hours.

As I walked toward the front of the train station, I noticed a dozen or more obvious travelers tucked inside their sleeping bags, stretched out on the cool, clean marbled floors of that rather immaculate station. It was totally fine and perfectly legal for me to sleep on the floor until sunrise — until shops reopened and business was in motion once again.

Sunrise revealed an extraordinary surprise: daylight flooding in through thirty-foot windows that were rounded at the top, allowing a breathtaking view of the snow-covered Alps that surrounded the city I had woken up in. I had no idea they were there while I was asleep. **What a truly magnificent thing to wake to — an immensely beautiful sight to behold!** Now I understood the sheer excitement those lovely American girls simply couldn't contain. And I, like them, had planned to stay three days and wound up staying for a full, refreshing week.

# Things to be Said with a Parisian Accent

Paris... the City of Lights... the City of Love. *Amour!* And what more could any romantic wanderer want but *amour*? Aren't we all romantics at heart while we wander through life with an unbridled sense of excitement and openness? Paris is so much more than wine and cheese, dark-roast coffee, savory croissants, and rich food smothered in flavorful sauces; more than lovely, affordable pensions with marbled pillars, colorfully tiled floors, and private balconies overlooking bustling open-air markets displaying perfectly placed, artfully arranged, exquisite, and delicious fruits and vegetables.

Paris is a city that has stirred the hearts and kindled the creative minds of so many poets, painters, musicians, and sculptors — an ideal breeding ground for hot-blooded bohemians and sensual intellectuals — *La vie boheme!* — the true historians, one might say. Paris is a city that encourages would-be writers to find themselves and forge their own "A Moveable Feast." Hemingway had his. And I was fiercely determined to keep finding and shaping the likes of my own, doing my damnedest to stay forever lost in the making of my own transportable banquet to carry with me throughout the course of my life! **The thing to remember about a moveable feast is that it's moving.**

My stay in Paris was unexpectedly extended due to a complete across-the-board transportation strike that included trains, planes, buses, boats, and taxis. For me that meant remaining in Paris a week or so longer than I had planned. And I can say, unequivocally, that there are far worse places one could get stuck than in the exquisitely romantic city of Paris in the early part of autumn.

> *"If you are lucky enough to have lived in Paris as a young man,*
> *then wherever you go for the rest of your life it stays with you,*
> *for Paris is a moveable feast."*
> *— Ernest Hemingway*

# British Notes and Scales

From railway to waterway — train to ferry — on route from Paris to Great Britain, where the roots of my mother tongue were aptly planted long ago. I'll say less about London than I thought I would, but I found it to be a breath of fresh air in so many ways. I was there for several weeks and it wasn't long enough. I'll do my best to list a few highlights before making the deliberate and purposefully promised leap that I've been edging us toward all along.

Hyde Park — Speakers Corner in particular, which I visited repeatedly while in Great Britain's winsome capital city; Camden Market; the River Thames; bohemian Soho; Piccadilly Circus; and the ever-iconic Abbey Road are among the places that left me with a rich and colorful assortment of lasting impressions. And I'd be remiss not to mention at least a couple of the plays I took in. I saw an award-winning production of *Jesus Christ Superstar* at the Criterion Theatre. And the dancing, moving, grand, uplifting, percussion-driven production of *Ipi Tombi* (Where Is the Girl) at Her Majesty's Theatre.

Leaving the theater located in the City of Westminster and taking the Underground, heading back to the Sussex Gardens apartment I was staying in — what a delightful surprise. The Tube was immaculate… no trash, graffiti, or sense of being less than safe. Quite a contrast from the Chicago subway system I was accustomed to back home. Of course "safe and clean" is a relative thing that could be debated. But by the comparison I couldn't help but make at that time, London's Underground was akin to a quaint and narrow moving palace compared to Chicago's let's just say less-than-pristine subway system.

London was lovely. I could have stayed longer, though something else was calling, and I had to abide.

*"There is a tide in the affairs of men.*

*Which, taken at the flood, leads on to fortune;*

*Omitted, all the voyage of their life*

*Is bound in shallows and in miseries.*

*On such a full sea are we now afloat,*

*And we must take the current when it serves,*

*Or lose our ventures."*

— William Shakespeare

# Returning to the Netherlands

After many magical, intermittently arduous months of being mostly on the move, it occurred to me that it might well be the ideal time to make my way back to the Netherlands. That was the intention I held in the back of my mind all along. My plan from the outset was to live in Amsterdam for an undetermined period of time. There was an ashram in Amsterdam that I knew about through my Kundalini yoga teacher in Chicago, and I decided it was time to go find it.

I had been on the move for weeks and weeks, away from my Midwestern roots for nine full months — three whole life-affirming trimesters — long enough to give birth to one's self, I suppose. Giving birth to ourselves tends to be simultaneously enlivening and tiring. We travel in order to revel in the new; to immerse ourselves in the soul-stretching, horizon-expanding benefits of continuous discovery. And yet all those thought-provoking wonders we encounter in the midst of world travel tend to become taxing at some point. The physical demands were beginning to wear on me. The few and far-between full night's sleep, burning more calories than I was taking in, and running low on money — that coalescence of practical facts contributed to my hard-to-ignore sense of fatigue.

# Time to Find the Ashram

I was told that I could find the chief (not an official title) of the ashram at the Golden Temple, a delightfully trendy vegetarian restaurant a few blocks south of Amsterdam's town square. I had no problem locating the Golden Temple restaurant, where I did indeed meet the head of the ashram — a tall, blue-eyed, red-bearded Scottish-American Sikh living a yogic lifestyle in the Netherlands. I was leaning quite heavily toward such a lifestyle as well back then... me, a slightly-less-tall, blue-eyed, light-brown-bearded, Italian-Irish-Russian-French, Catholic-Jewish, American-born, body-building Buddhist with a Jungian background and an irrepressible eagerness to explore different customs while immersing myself in a multitude of deep-rooted disciplines.

I sat at a table with the red-bearded man I just described, drinking spicy-sweet Yogi tea and talking about our travels, among other things. He had recently visited the Golden Temple in Amritsar, India — the actual temple as opposed to the quaint little Amsterdam restaurant bearing its name. We talked about my yoga teacher in Chicago, whom he knew well and undoubtedly held in high regard. I told him about the intention carried with me throughout my nine months of travel and my readiness to make it my reality. I conveyed my desire to live in the ashram, continue to study and practice Kundalini yoga, and see where it might lead. He smiled, bowed his head in approval of all that I said, and asked me to meet him back at the restaurant the following day so we could speak further and sort a few things that still needed to be sorted.

I went back in the afternoon the following day, tired, hungry, and hoping to hear what I wanted to hear, which was simply: Yes... come, stay, study, and be part of what you've wanted to be part of. I sat at a table peering out the window at my potential new home. A few minutes later I was joined once again by the tall, red-bearded head of the ashram. He sat down and smiled warmly, telling me he had spoken with my yoga teacher in Chicago earlier that day. My teacher more than merely vouched for me; he said I was clearly one of the most promising students he'd been privileged to teach. Needless to say, I was in!

When we come face to face with the manifestation of any long-held fantasy, something's gotta give! I'm not suggesting that all aspects of fantasy need to be weeded out and/or decisively severed from what we deem to be "real." Our realities are shaped, in part, by the ebb and flow of human emotions impacting our perceptions, which continue to shift accordingly. We can be both lost in and led by the reverie of those *avant-garde* fantasies, respectfully sheltered in one of the impeccably decorated guest rooms of the psyche. However, our fantasies rarely, if ever, come close to matching the reality largely prompted by an array of ostensibly flawless ruminations.

When something we've long imagined and thought we wanted is viewed through the lens of real-life experience, it tends to look, sound, and feel quite different from what we had in mind. And if it turns out to be something we're not truly suited for, we raise our glasses and drink a toast to disillusionment! Disillusionment is but a blessing in the semblance of disappointment. And disappointment is a natural and inevitable part of any genuine human life. In order to honor our own uniquely personal evolution we must be discerning enough to identify and appropriately dis — as in dismiss — our illusions. If we aren't disillusioned along the way, we tend to be left with our illusions intact, and a reality too porous to build upon.

The days and weeks to follow were rather telling, if not enlightening, to say the least. I didn't mind climbing the steep, narrow, ladder-like staircase or sleeping on the floor of one of the fourth floor bedrooms. Nor did I have any problem rising at 4:00am, taking an ice-cold shower, and making my way downstairs for morning meditation, typically followed by a rigorous, vigorous yoga class. And I had no objection to washing dishes at the Golden Temple restaurant in exchange for room and board at the ashram. However, I did have a problem attempting to think within the confines of a singular belief system — a philosophical disorder that can only be ordered through adventurous openness... a condition I've invariably opted not to cure.

The ashram became another stop — an eight-week stay along the way. It was a place to rest, recoup, and resurrect my renewed spirit of adventure. It takes time to reconfigure the "me" we are at the start of any extended, intermittently arduous, eye-opening journey with the "me" we are continuously in the midst of becoming along our arousing geographical routes. I had been on the move for nearly one year collecting a rich assortment of synergistic story seeds I now felt ready to nurture in my hometown soil.

*"Your soul knows the geography of your destiny. Your soul alone
has the map of your future; therefore you can trust this indirect,
oblique side of yourself. If you do, it will take you where you need
to go, but more important it will teach you a kindness of
rhythm in your journey."*
— John O'Donohue

# Heading Home

After nearly a year of travel, exploration, and a wide array of largely welcomed discoveries, the enlivening rhythm of my journey was calling me back to my good old American Midwestern roots. I had left my home, my city, my country... family, friends, what I knew, what I thought I knew, and what I had come to consider a tad too familiar. I left my Windy City hometown with a sophomoric eagerness to see, touch, taste, conquer, devour, and take time to savor enough to truly become the man of the world I believed I needed to be.

I flew home from Holland, leaving delicious old Amsterdam after a two-month stay in order to revisit that beloved Windy City I was born in. After being back home in Chicago for less than two full days, a question emerged from the depths of my psyche — from the hub of my soul; a question that might have sounded simple enough on any other day, but on that day — my second day home after a lengthy journey that included sights, sounds, scents, and a variety of flavors I tasted and savored in thirteen countries, on three different continents — the question that took hold of my awareness and wouldn't let go was anything but simple or weightless. The question was: **"What do I now know for certain?"** And the only answer I came to — the only answer my mind was willing to provide me with — was... **Nothing!**

That powerfully weighty one-word answer was an answer my man-of-the-world ego wasn't prepared for or ready to accept. I had seen quite a bit in those last eleven months. I had met and conversed with people from dozens of different countries — some that were fluent in ten or more tongues. I had shared food and stories with warm-hearted strangers in lands I had merely imagined a year before. Now that I had slept, dreamt, breathed, stepped, danced, and lived in many regions of the world, what, if anything, did I know unequivocally? What did I now know for certain? No matter how many times I asked, the answer was the same. Regardless of how I framed, reframed, or attempted to rephrase that provocatively pressing question, the answer remained precisely the same: Nothing! Nothing was the only soulfully open and honest answer my mind would allow.

# The Revelatory Nature of Knowing Nothing At All

Knowing nothing, if only briefly, momentarily, is not necessarily a great and powerful revelation. But knowing you know nothing while steeped in the present can, in fact, lead to a deep, undeniable sense of emancipation that can't be denied, overlooked, or casually dismissed. It all comes down to a willful embrace. The instant I stopped shielding myself from the inherent wisdom dwelling within that one-word answer, something shifted — everything changed. And with that change, the weight of the world was promptly lifted from my Windy-City-born-and-raised broad shoulders. Perception shapes, defines, fuels, and influences all that we see, know, sense, and comprehend.

With a seemingly subtle, albeit purposeful shift, came a serendipitous sense of acceptance; and my acceptance was the very key that opened a door allowing the spirit of euphoria to take hold and guide my awareness for days to follow. And it wasn't as if I knew something I hadn't known a moment prior — something I could say I now knew with utter certainty; it was simply a matter of my no longer minding that "nothing" anymore. What started out as a heavy problem I thought I needed to solve turned into a weightless realization that didn't need to be fixed or altered in any way. Somehow everything seemed inexplicably perfect. And for the next three days that followed that epiphanous shift, I'm not entirely certain my feet touched the ground. **This was the most magnificent nothing in the world one could never imagine!**

After soaring for nearly four days, hovering over familiar streets and well-known sidewalks, I saw an old friend while waiting at a bus stop on Sheridan Road, about a block from Lake Michigan near Loyola University: Ruvane Gold — my delightfully disheveled storyteller friend.

"Aah — you've been on a long journey," Ruvane exclaimed. "When did you get back?"

"About four days ago," I answered.

"How long were you away?"

"I was away for almost a year."

"Where did you go? What did you see? I want to hear all about your journey; your travels. Come — let's sit, drink coffee, and talk about the world... this crazy, amazing, beautifully mysterious, perfectly topsy-turvy world! Come! Come! I want to hear everything."

Conveniently enough, that bus stop I had been waiting at was in close proximity to Cindy Sue's, a neighborhood restaurant we'd both been to many times.

"Coffee sounds great," I said. "I'd love to catch up and tell you a bit about where I've been."

"A bit," said Ruvane in a playfully disapproving tone. "I want to know everything! I want to hear everything... where you've been, what you did, what you saw. You must tell me everything," Ruvane said with a fiercely sincere sense of interest.

"Okay," I said, "I'd love to tell you all about my travels. But I have to tell you something first." We were now seated at a booth in the restaurant. Our friendly waitress was quick to pour us each a fresh cup of mediocre coffee while I began to tell my storyteller friend about my recent realization.

Ruvane was a storyteller by profession. That's what he did for a living; it's what he loved — what defined him and made him who he was. You could catch him on TV, in the middle of the night, around 2:00 or 3:00am on WGN Channel Nine. He told Hasidic tales and old-world myths from many wisdom traditions round the globe. And he told Sufi stories — captivating folk tales and enticing fables of Nasrudin and the Caravan of Dreams.

So there I was, seated at a booth in a greasy-spoon restaurant on the north side of Chicago, facing my storyteller friend who made it abundantly clear that he was eager to hear my newly acquired real-life stories.

"Something happened," I told him, "a couple days after I got home. A question floated into the forefront of my mind and took root there, refusing to budge or sway a bit before getting answered. The question was 'What do I now know for certain?' And the only answer I kept coming to was... 'Nothing!' I kept asking the same question over and over because I wasn't ready to embrace and accept such a weighty, one-word answer. I mean, how do you process nothing? How do you reconcile the emphatic longing to know and understand everything with the painfully unyielding awareness of knowing nothing at all?"

I continued. "Is there a proper perspective to put that into?... because nothing doesn't leave much room for adjustment — nothing means there's nothing to adjust to, extrapolate from, build upon, or extol the unknown virtues of. What I experienced the other day after nearly a full year of travel was a deep, profound, initially painful realization that I truly knew nothing! My whole life, including all of my studies, all that I've read, and all that I've experienced thus far in this life — all of the places I've been, especially within the last eleven months, all the eyes I've looked into while engaged in conversation, all I thought I knew for certain, once upon a time — led me to realize that **I really know nothing... nothing at all!"**

My old friend Ruvane, who had been sitting in respectful silence keeping direct eye contact with me the entire time while listening intently to what I needed to say, suddenly jolted back against the dark-red Naugahyde-covered booth as if being pushed back by an impactful surprise. Then slowly leaning forward, as close as the booth between us would allow, his intense brown eyes still fixed on mine, in a crescendo of impregnated silence, took a long, slow, deep, full breath... and said, **"BRAGGART!"**

We both broke into spontaneous and uncontrollable laughter. And after our delightful belly laughs had settled into the aftermath of simple joy, Ruvane looked at me with that older, wiser, storyteller smile and said, **"Don't you know... that knowing nothing is the very foundation of truly knowing anything at all?"**

> *"The real treasure, that which we all seek, is never very far:*
> *there is no need to seek it in a distant place, for it is buried within*
> *our own hearts. And yet, there is this strange and persistent fact,*
> *that only after a journey in a distant region, in a new land,*
> *the way to that treasure becomes clear."*
> — *Heinrich Zimmer*

# CHAPTER 2

# Rituals, Discipline, and Creative Imagination

# The Narrative of Then and Now

"Once upon a time" can't compete with or be compared to the amaranthine unfolding of our actual everyday lives! Then again… sometimes it can! When the "here and now" is less than to our liking, "once upon a time" becomes a welcome distraction or creative diversion from the ever-relentless moment at hand. Sometimes we need a sound escape plan — a robust rerouting of our seemingly lackluster narrative — in which awareness is stifled and our thoughts are at risk of becoming as barren as an endless desert, void of dreams.

There are moments that seem like days, when I feel as if I'm a century or two behind the times or an imaginative aeon ahead of them. Every part of history has been perfectly flawed — rife with the wonders, joys, and agonies of "real life" — just as every passing day is undoubtedly touched by eternity. And sometimes "once upon a time" can be a useful tool in cutting a path through the labyrinth of misguided thoughts and disjointed memories of better or worse times.

Once upon a time the world was a story, told by a child, to a woman or a man. Our sentient recollections are part of the primal retelling of this miraculous ongoing tale. We think in parallels, speak in parables, and dream in timeless paradigms. Once upon a time we were breathless, restless, and resolute! Courageous determination was our internal road map, and inviolable desire was the indelible chart we carried with us.

Once upon a time I was the World's Greatest Lover — and Don Juan was my apprentice, despite the fact that we lived in different times. Once upon a time I was a warrior, a king, a beggar, a philosopher, a wanderer, a thief. I was a Bedouin on horseback, riding like a whirlwind through the desert of my dreams. Once upon a time I was a noetic fisherman, casting imaginative nets from my hand-carved canoe, tossing them into those murky rivers mystics swim in after being exiled for the umpteenth time for the noble crime of simply not fitting in. Once upon a time I was a heroic explorer of old and new worlds — a romantic wayfarer using wonder as my reliable road map — and passion was the only compass I carried with me. I was a shameless and incurable wonderer, a playwright in my own right, acting out every fantastically impassioned scene from the courtyard of my creative imagination.

If I were to tell you that I began writing before I was born, and that I painted hieroglyphs onto uterine walls, I wouldn't be lying. My memoirs began before my first breath, long before my loving mother ousted me from the perfectly warm, aqueous realm of her womb. Time, after all, is an ongoing mystery; chronology is merely a playful way of attempting to compartmentalize that which is eternal. There are conspicuous differences between hard, fast rules and creative rituals. And I tend to favor the latter. Thank goodness for my spirited insurgency, without which I wouldn't exist. Thank goodness for those fiery stars that fed and nurtured my rebellious nature, the RNA of my robust awareness, the DNA of my poetic point of view. Thank goodness for my resistance to mediocrity that allowed me to build a rollicking immunity to the poisonous misconceptions of the day while staying widely open to the beautiful and immeasurable mystery.

Every age has been "Golden," fire-baked, covered in mud, and seeded with colorful visions. We're all in search of a sense of belonging to a place and time we feel whole, alive, and fully aligned with while we grapple with abstracts, wrestle the present, and entertain the perpetually unfolding moment at hand.

We are merely the impassioned intermediaries of the thoughts we tap into and momentarily honor as our own. We are more or less prismatic reflections of the future we view from one of the many hilltops of our pasts — rhythmic writer-poet-philosophers prompted by a heartbeat! We are the breath of fresh air we've wanted all along — the breath of life we tend to take for granted time and again. What we inhale and exhale every day is an integral part of those ancient and enduring winds of change we pray for and avoid intermittently while moving from dream to dream with the sentient swiftness of shooting stars hurling fiery sonnets through the kaleidoscopic darkness of the cosmos.

# On Being an Outcast

Okay! Alright! I get it. I understand why I am an outcast, an outlaw, an outlying linguist on the outskirts of societal norms. I know why I've been repeatedly banished from nearly every organized group I tried in vain to fit into, and why I've proudly ousted myself from all the others.

How audacious of me to fully abandon any and every halfhearted attempt at successfully blending in with any group, gang, or congregation I couldn't truly connect with or fit into. I've always been a bit of a rascal, a rebel, a gypsy-hearted vagabond — sadly/ecstatically dancing along the obstreperous edges of creative exile.

I am an outcast, an outlaw — persona fucking non grata by default! This is my fate, my destiny, my just reward for having committed the unforgivable sin of living my own life deliberately, decidedly, and with all the unbridled passion I could muster. I've been shunned, avoided, dismissed, overlooked, and given the colloquial cold shoulder for living a largely unrelatable life and for knowing that "these," indeed, are the days, as opposed to "those" so many I know continue to cling to while nonchalantly disowning the NOW and routinely dismissing the moment at hand with their tenaciously disavowing wish to trade the lively, sensate, preeminent present for some mostly imagined, largely synthetic, all-too-tenuous once upon a time.

# Dead Poets, Live Poets, and Mr. Thoreau

I turned on my Samsung big-screen HD Smart TV the other night, and these soul-stirring words filled more than the screen; they filled the vitalizing, wide-open fullness of my being:

> *"I went into the woods because I wanted to live deliberately...I wanted to live deep and suck out all the marrow of life! To put to rest all that was not life...And not, when I came to die, discover that I had not lived."*
> *— Henry David Thoreau*

My impulse was to press the pause button — freeze those enlivening words made large across my TV screen — in order to savor the rousing emotion and depth of meaning fully embedded in every pulsating syllable of Henry David Thoreau's written expression. That single paragraph is a rich, succinct, and empowering summation of the majestic life and inspiring work of Mr. Thoreau.

That heart-gripping paragraph covering nearly the entire screen of my big ol' TV was one of the many enthralling scenes from the movie *Dead Poets Society*, starring the inimitable, much loved, much missed Robin Williams.

Thoreau's words, Robin's no-less-than-brilliant performance, the film in its beautifully heart-wrenching totality... life, death, poetry, suicide... time, eternity, *carpe diem* (seize the day), the urge to act, fire in the belly, the undeniable impulse to live!... so much condensed in one tiny paragraph: meaning, purpose, divine possibility, the courage to go into — and come out of — the woods. All of that and so much more, simultaneously emerging in my heart and mind, bubbling up from the hub of my soul, awakened by a compelling paragraph penned more than a century and a half ago.

I unfroze the screen, letting those words roll away in order to watch a bit more of the movie. I watched Mr. Keating weep as he read the handwritten inscription on the title page of a weighty volume entitled *Five Centuries of Verse*. I continued to watch, knowing it was only a matter of time before I'd be weeping, too. I decided to rewind back to H. D. T.'s words, paused them again, got up to grab my Amazon Fire, opened it eagerly, touched on the camera app, and clicked a few shots of Thoreau's electrified words painted across the screen of my TV.

I was flooded by a deep, wide river of thoughts fused with timeless human emotion... Dead Poets. A truly giving and gifted actor, comedian, and man who opted for suicide. The film lives on. The words are alive. The nature of art — the art of nature. Creativity has the potential to live for centuries, rendering thoughts and feelings alive and well again and again. Passion. Expression. One precious paragraph frozen in time, thawed in the fiery heart of eternity, dripping, seeping, and divinely flooding the mind of a poet in the woods of his or her own living room.

Seize the moment. Seize the day. Say whatever you want and know you need to say. The breath of life remains in perpetual motion. Breathe in, breathe out; let it in, let it out. Life is fleeting. Life is eternal — a grand performance or perennial pause; periphrastic phrases romantically woven with primordial yarn onto a teleological tapestry; the immaculate imagery of wonder and innocence; a testament to Here and Now, I and Thou, More or Less; the kinetic abundance of WHAT IN THE WHOLE BLOODY WORLD IS ENOUGH? Modernity. Technology. Mediocrity and rebellion. Cell phones, computers, iPad 4, Amazon Fire, Smart TV... television was nonexistent when Thoreau's words were first published in 1854, more than a century before I was born, and yet there they were the other night, painted across my TV screen like diminutive angels in the guise of verse; like a soulful apparition graciously emerging from the holy, heartfelt vespers of a lifelong dream.

# What Must Come First

This must come first: the deliberate writing away of my demons of doubt. This is the order I choose, the steady progression I opt to inscribe. This is where the road begins but never ends, while following the trajectory of these fleeting thoughts, soaring dreams, and moving visions spilling profusely from the ethereal mind onto the heretofore empty page. This is where I come and go to flush out all those sacred ghosts and to catch any naysayers who might have slipped most stealthily into my psyche in the thick of day or dark of night.

I come here naked and ready for battle, wielding my silver-tipped pen like a true linguistic warrior, chanting, "Come out and fight; it's a good day to die," while honoring life! I come here to rid myself of uninvited guests and to light a candle for the sake of passion, purpose, and those potent possibilities that follow me like explorative children offering guidance to the man I've become. These, then, are my coordinates — my ephemeral lines of latitude and longitude crossing the threshold of creative imagination and marking the prime meridian with preeminent octopus ink. It's all about adventure, I've heard — I've said, though I seem to have forgotten to remember what it means.

These pointillistic feasibilities keep capturing my attention, inveigling my awareness, and sparking more than casual curiosity. This spotted, dotted, speckled perspective is a rather evocative way to see directly into the present from the spellbinding wavelengths of the liminal past. This is more than the copulation of spirited phrases intended to seed the hope of giving birth to a naked conception covered in the fertile blood of life. It isn't ink that stains these pages after all, but the amniotic fluid of my co-created fate.

# My Delightfully Ritualized Everyday Life as a Writer

It's all about ritual — every silly, bloody, seriously delirious, calmingly disquieting, delightfully disruptive, undeniably centering, creatively enabling step of the way! My ritual begins by literally leaping from bed — forward, from the foot of our bed. I've been employing that ritual for well over a decade. Leaping forward from bed is a far better way to start the day than reluctantly dragging one leg over the edge and letting it dangle while deciding whether or not it's really worth it. I practiced that rather common ritual for a time, and I can say without a doubt that leaping from bed is a far better way to begin. (There isn't a footboard at the end of my bed, allowing free, unfettered access to the floor beyond it.)

Leaping forward into the day has been and continues to be the perfect way for me to greet the day. But let me go back to bed for a moment in order to provide an unembellished, albeit fully detailed description of my actual everyday leaping-from-bed ritual.

First I remove the covers and pull them under as opposed to over my body. Then, while lying on my back watching daylight dance on the ceiling above me, I take a deep, full, benevolent breath — the breath of life! I take a few more affirmative breaths and silently say *yes!* to myself. Yes to life ever fresh and new. Yes to openness, eagerness, passion, purpose, and possibility. Yes to this new day, this gift, this opportunity. Yes to courage, clarity, strength, and wholeness. Yes to adventure, discovery, friendship, connection, reflection, and the language of life. Yes to vision, gratitude, forgiveness, fulfillment! Then I lift my arms and legs about eighty degrees above my firm, comfy bed, hands and feet pointing forward toward the end of my bed, while listening attentively to that inner voice saying, "Go forward and be the blessing you're meant to be. Go forward, in wholeness, and be the blessing that I am!" That is precisely what I think and say to myself as I leap forward from bed every morning.

And after going to the bathroom and brushing my teeth (those beautiful little mundane rituals), it's time to prepare my morning coffee, the elixir of the writer's life. Coffee — that creatively fragrant, dark, delectable, blessed brew. First I choose the beans. I tend to have at least two or three different organic, dark-roast varieties on hand on any given day. I select the beans and measure the number of scoops to the ratio of water — typically enough for two full cups when I'm making coffee for only myself. I measure the water in my glass decanter. Then carry the decanter of water to my living room window; open the window fully; step as close to the window as I possibly can, standing with my nose an inch or less away from the screen; and take a deep, slow, purposeful breath — **Air**. I then lift my water-filled decanter above my head — **Water**. I lift and hold it up toward the sun — **Fire**. I align my vision with those well-rooted plum trees and glistening evergreens before panning the landscape — the fertile ground and flowing hills that rise from this amazing topography — **Earth**. I bring all the elements and my awareness of them into the water I will use to brew my morning coffee — the elements of life, the elements of my aliveness. And before carrying those blessed waters back to my kitchen, I take a step back away from, but still facing, my window and lift them over my head once again to affirm the waters of life, the fluidity of life, the flow of life — the healing waters, holy waters, flowing waters, knowing waters, blessed waters, creative waters, connecting waters, reflecting waters, plentiful waters, purposeful waters, rejuvenating waters, life-giving waters.

Those are the waters I then use to brew my morning coffee, the elixir of the gods and goddesses I call upon to entice and invite the muses to come sit at my table while I write. When the coffee's done dripping into my glass carafe, I pour a cup, add a bit of dark brown sugar, a touch of organic half-and-half, and a grateful sense of wholeness. Now I'm ready to write!

I begin with pen and notebook — freehand at my writing table ala Julia Cameron's glorious "Morning Pages." I owe Julia a great debt of gratitude, not merely for her magnificent books, most notably *The Artists Way*, which I had the great good fortune of finding a couple decades ago, but also for the joyful privilege of taking part in half-a-dozen workshops she taught here on the West Coast many memorable moons ago. Thank you, Julia, for inspiring this magnanimous morning ritual that continues to shape, guide, and motivate my extraordinary-ordinary daily writing practice.

Writing is an art, a privilege, a discipline, and a continuous source of discovery. And discoveries are rarely, if ever, made without a courageous and impassioned sense of adventure. Writing is a kind of yoga of the psyche, a tai chi of the spirit; it's the "Zen of the Pen," the gymnastics of the focused mind, and the odyssey that lends itself to boundless creativity and unbridled expression.

My writing space is my holy ground, my island paradise, my fertile and fruitful tropical retreat. This is where it begins, begins, and begins again but never ends; this is where I find myself — and lose myself repeatedly. This is my poetic port in the great storm of life, my mostly mellifluous linguistic haven — the amicable belly of the literary whale. This is where I swim or drown on arid land and saunter as well as dance atop those tempestuous metaphorical waves. This is the metaphysical uterus of pure awareness, the mythological womb through which I give birth to myself.

My writing table is my veritable lifeboat, made from mahogany — my humanistic hovercraft, my tiny little rowboat in the wide-open waters of the world. This is where I get to be Ishmael, Odysseus, and The Old Man, as well as the sad boy at sea. This is where I kneel in the dust of faraway lands and ride into battle beside Don Quixote while respectfully bowing to the enigmatic shadow of myself. This is my magnificent mahogany altar upon which mediocrity is consistently sacrificed for the sake of getting in touch with the sublime.

On my writing table, on any given day, you're bound to find a variety of sacred, fertile, sensate things such as leaves I've collected along the way, pine cones I've lifted from the ground after a windstorm, or an assortment of stones — plain, precious, and probably worthless to anyone other than me. They are invaluable to me because I know where and when and how I found them — or they found me.

These simple stones that rest on my writing table have stories to tell, and I am an eager listener with an impassioned interest, yearning to hear them. And sometimes, on those days when virtually nothing seems solid, I'll take hold of one of those stones and allow it to help me get grounded.

Near those stones you can see my porcelain sun with its hand-painted face, those inquisitive eyes glancing into the light of my own, smiling at the world I keep getting lost in. Oh, and my lovely porcelain, hand-painted heart, deep, dark purple, and able to be opened. And if you do decide to open it, you'll find fortunes, as in narrow bits of paper plucked from individually wrapped cookies. And on those narrow bits of paper you'll find words, typically printed in red or green ink, saying things like "You stand in your own light. Make it shine." In addition to those fortunes you'll find ash — remnants of sage I have burned to purify the air and offer my thoughts a smoky, earth-scented baptism while setting the stage for creative surprises and fortunate spills. And mixed with copious fortunes and medicinal ash there are seeds from my magnificent mimosa tree that I can see and touch and stand in awe of from my balcony to the world.

On and all around my writing table there are plentiful images, paintings, prints, and photos I keep in my line of vision — bold inspirations drawing me in and conspicuously urging me to dance onto the page. And always, in the center — in the heart and hub of my ever-encouraging table for one — stands a candle, a simple, quintessential symbol of light. I always light a candle to honor my impassioned quest and desire for fire and light. I light a candle in order to reconnect and recollect the dream this all began with.

*"Life begins with the dream and proceeds outward from there."*
*— C. G. Jung*

I light a candle so that I might remember that otherwise forgotten dream. I light a candle to ritualize and romanticize this timeless, intermittently arduous, albeit wondrous and rewarding odyssey I've come to recognize as my Everyday Life as a Writer!

# Ode to those Artists I've loved for so Long

An ode to those artists I've loved for so long . . .
An epode to Van Gogh; monologue for Monet,
A ballad for Blake,
Sonnet for Thoreau and an epyllion for Emerson.

This is my pitiless way of giving back to those
Ghosts I serve tea to in the great flood of daylight.

They come; they visit, they sit at my table --
Attempting to reenact a mummers' play that
Can't be rehearsed or ever acted out the same way twice.

Like a banshee suddenly deciding to sing a love
Song in lieu of a wailing warning of imminent death --
Realizing Life is imminent too.

French horns in the background -- flutes on the
Hill chimes in the treetops, lutes in the shadows,
Marimba in the wind -- and those silhouetted
Sopranos attempting to harmonize with tentative
Tenors wearing African daisies in their nightshade lapels.

Oh, to write an ode to the artist I've become . . .
Just sit down, sit here, and simply write!

Write until there's nothing left to remember --
Until those cacophonous whispers in the guise
Of silence become a symphony of open secrets.

Write until those ripe plums fall like bitter
Cherries from the wind-brushed branches
Of a tall metaphorical peach tree -- and
Until those pumpkin-scented anthologies
Are willing to reveal their anonymous names.

Just write about what you know -- what you
Don't know, what you want to know, need to know,
And could never fully know in a thousand lifetimes.

Write like the wind, like the sea and all those
Lively creatures hidden
Beneath those salty, seductive, tumultuous waves.
Write from where you are -- from what you are,
For who you are and wish to become all the more.

Write about those bakers that rise in the middle
Of the night -- slowly
Like the dough they use for baking our daily bread.

Write about those daring mountaineers and
Seditious ventriloquists -- putting words in
The mouths of otherwise mindless puppets.

Write from the landscape-dreamscape
That shapes, feeds and defines your perception.

Write about what can't be written -- and
About that song you started but can't seem to finish.

Write about the debris on all those rooftops --
The organic kindling that must be
Cleared before the fire season begins again.

Write about all those allergies you've outgrown --
And the ambition you seem to no longer have either.

Write about those lucid dreams that took you
By storm in the midst of broad daylight --
While traipsing through the wilderness of postponed desires.

Write about those lingering smells of burning leaves --
Within those beautifully turbulent Midwestern falls

That filled my senses and fed my rapacious longing
For more than what my hometown could possibly offer.

Write about those broken promises -- the crumbling
Infrastructure, brittle visions,
Borrowed intentions, the stolen lifestyle and amassed burnt
offerings.

Write a simple recipe; three parts shadow,
Four parts light and a dash of audacity --
Served raw, uncooked, warm and bloody.

Write about those chocolate-coated nightmares and
Honey-glazed torments -- thinly spread across stale bread.

Write -- one -- fucking -- paragraph . . . an epitaph
For the you that you buried before you were born.
Write an apology or an appraisal of your true self-worth.

Write your own name, for heavens sake!
Write the stories you don't want to write.
Write your acceptance speech -- and your letter of resignation.
Write those memoirs no one else in the world could
possibly write.
Then write them again -- in mythological terms.

Write until your hearts content, or until it explodes
From the pressure of unexpressed passion.
Write until the cows come home -- until the chickens
Come to roost -- until the dove delivers that long-awaited
olive branch.

Write about the utter irrelevance of
Doing nearly-anything-other-than-write.

Write from your unrelenting rebellious nature --
From that perfectly determined spirit that will not be denied!

Write for your life -- from the soul of yourself . . . from the
The YOU that simply will not permit anything to
Diminish, derail or recklessly squander your full-hearted
Efforts, ability and burning desire to fucking write!
Fucking right!

# The Choreography of the In-Between

I suppose I could call my largely private, deeply personal sense of purgatory "the intermittent anguish of the in-between." It's never that easy to give it a name when I need to. Calling it angst would be too simple; agony, a tad too dramatic. Whatever I call it, it's mine — and I'll own it and honor it as best I can. It's not the tired old fire-and-brimstone fantasy of sulfur-heavy air invading the atmosphere, but a rather pragmatic quest for the soul of genuine faith. It is my selfishly altruistic exploration of unfettered creativity and largely undiluted self-expression.

I'm between thoughts right now... between worlds right now... between the seemingly solid, well-anchored perspectives and those perpetually fluid, momentarily lucid points of view. This is akin to standing naked near the shores of the Aegean, the Atlantic, or the big, blue Pacific, eavesdropping on an ancient conversation between land and sea. I feel as if I'm dancing round the edges of Dante's *Divine Comedy*, staying faithful to my own opportunity to say and do something of value while I can. There is so much to sort through — thoughts, memories, insightful dreams, and inspiring recollections. I feel as if I'm sinking-floating somewhere between Kurosawa's *Dreams* and my own, somewhere between Dante's forest dark and Van Gogh's maddening *Wheatfield with Crows*, here in the middle of this profound poiesis of haunting shadows and continuously fervent symbiotic sounds, giving rise to the music I've chosen to accompany the periodic absence of chronology.

These collective sounds, inner and outer, ambient and otherwise, remind me that I can dance and that I must! This, then, is the spirited choreography of the in-between — between the minimal and the limitless, between the bridled and the boundless, between a lackadaisical state of limbo and the periodically longed for limelight, allowing others to get but a glimpse of who we truly are while on this enigmatic oasis of all that is. I am here, both by chance and by circumstance. And this is where I've decided to throw down the gauntlet, slapping myself in the face with the glove of true desire and challenging my dilemma to a duel! This is where I fully intend to take hold of chaos and shake it into submission to a vision more to my liking.

Chaos stirs in the heart of creation, but the heart of creation is a multichambered mystery — a multidimensional realm of rhythmic, blood-pumping awareness. This is the heart that we all live in, consciously or otherwise, deliberately or by default. All that we do and do not do amount to the choices we make from moment to moment. And those moment-by-moment choices we make each day have an impact and an influence on the shaping of the stories that breathe life into our destinies by bringing our destinies to life!

# CHAPTER 3

# Reflections on Challenge and the Need to Push Through

# Reflections on Solitude from a Pen Pusher's Perspective

Solitude is part of the conservation of our innermost landscape, where we plant ourselves and continue to nurture what we wish and want and need to grow.

Solitude is the antithesis of loneliness — if and when we truly love the one we're with when we're alone.

Solitude is the wilderness guide we faithfully follow through the thicket of our fertile mind — the revenant we run with or from repeatedly.

Solitude is the ravenous wolf that might devour us if we dare to see ourselves too clearly.

Solitude is what we return to in order to baptize our psyche when the world goes dry.

Solitude is an epic battle between spontaneity and the overly planned; between the commonsensical "both feet on the ground" approach and a "taking aim at the stars" ideology.

Solitude is where the noble clash between tepid acquiescence and fiery rebellion takes place, face to face with those two apparently opposing sides of one's self.

Solitude is where we brush moondust from the aura of our innate understanding.

Solitude is where we take hold of our existential Etch A Sketch, turn it upside down, and shake it vigorously for the sake of a fresh, clean slate.

Solitude is where the ebb and tide of our innermost river engages in conversation with a systematic dam.

Solitude is our solemn prayer for true connection — the midwife of our sacred and most guarded dreams.

Solitude is our ship in the night guided by stars flickering in a sea of darkness.

Solitude is the beast we learn to tame for the sake of befriending our shadow, thus allowing our unseen side to guide us toward our co-created destiny.

Solitude is the childhood friend we tend to neglect but can never forget.

Solitude is simply a single page of my ethereal diary, feverishly written with my quixotic quill upon *trompe l'œil* clouds that convince us they hold fire.

Solitude is the great seductress — the exotic and quixotic temptress luring language into her bed.

Solitude is the symphony of continuous birth conducted by the midwife of our sacred and most highly guarded desires, visions, and dreams.

Solitude is the soliloquy we recite to the wind while spitting orange seeds into the waters of the womb in the world of pure awareness.

Solitude is where we face our faithful flaws and immaculate imperfections and laugh but a little at our own sadness.

Solitude is the soul mate many renounce repeatedly yet return to time and again.

Solitude is a synergistic joust between juxtaposed opposites coming into alignment at the speed of our true sound!

Solitude is forgiveness in the semblance of something else — an epic battle between loneliness and perfect union.

Solitude is the periscope we look through from the bottom of the soul — a sacred samba between land and sea.

The open secret is that we crave solitude for the sake of keeping in touch. We seek connection in our cherished hours of creative isolation wherein our most intimate conversations are permitted and encouraged to take place. Solitude is the gift we unwrap in the presence of a friend or stranger we've known our entire life.

# Attack of the Ever-Undying Clichés

At the outset of my ongoing journey, I was captured by a gang of Latin phrases. I was compelled at first light by *carpe diem*, and in my eagerness to take hold of it, it began to slip away.

*Carpe noctem* (seize the night) whispered a nocturnal spirit in the guise of a nightmarish nightingale singing into the darkness surrounding the nearly full moon while the night raven cried *mea culpa*!

I searched for the center between night and day, or a still point I could leap from. I sensed something deeper than my own vanity — something more profound than singing naked in the rain for the sake of bread and entertainment.

*Acta non verba* (actions, not words) uttered a silhouette, halfway hidden in an old-growth forest few can see for the trees. As I stepped closer, deeper, the stars got brighter and my path grew darker. I could barely see the back of my own hand, a thing I thought I knew so well. I was lost. And daylight was still a million miles away. I couldn't even remember what I was looking for. And if I were to remember, what good would it do? I ambled on nevertheless, a bit less aimless than I had felt an hour before.

Then the noise began as I found myself surrounded by a troublesome troupe of undying clichés. The commander was the first to speak, telling me — reminding me, attempting to sway me — with the all-to-dubious fact that ignorance is bliss. With my rebellious nature still fully intact, I stood my ground, telling my interrogator, "I wasn't convinced." Then the others were ordered to chime in, one after the other, in rapid succession.

Better safe than sorry. There's no time like the present. Another day, another dollar. Actions speak louder than words. Ashes to ashes. All in due time. Anything goes. As the crow flies, all talk and no action, at the end of the day, at the crack of dawn, ass backwards, at the end of my rope, you can't judge a book by its cover, the apple doesn't fall far from the tree, love is blind, you can't please them all, what doesn't kill you makes you stronger.

I felt myself growing weaker; my eyes getting glazed. I wasn't sure I could withstand much more. Then I raised my head; took a long, full breath; and shouted, "THE GRASS IS ALWAYS GREENER ON WHATEVER SIDE I STAND ON!" And immediately all those loud clichés were silenced.

# Benefit of the Doubt

Doubt is a checkpoint — a weigh station at the border between our dark and weighty imaginations and the lighter, brighter possibilities we've yet to let in.

Doubt could be our sure-footed Sherpa in the guise of our own opaque shadow, safely guiding snow-blind seekers, writers, poets, artists — people — through an avalanche of useless and inaccurate information.

Doubt is the magnetic center of our internal compass, permitting our instinctual needle to point us toward and realign us with our own true north.

Doubt is the unconscious seeding of self-made clouds deliberately obscuring a wide array of creative options we've remained either unaware of or habitually afraid to embrace.

Doubt is the dull, gray shelter we choose to hide in when the light of day threatens to expose us — an emotionally synthesized internal sun-block guarding us from those life-enhancing rays of impassioned wonder.

Doubt is the antidote to our addiction to certainty and our tenuous sense of security. Like those wise old Irish poets say: "A false sense of security is the only kind there is."

Doubt allows us to reexamine what we've overlooked and/or taken for granted in order to discover something new if we're willing to.

Doubt may well be more ally than enemy; a far better friend than any false sense of certainty.

Doubt can act as a catalyst for or conduit to disillusionment by permitting us to let go of what we thought we needed to believe we knew for certain.

Doubt is the impolite greeter who stands in the doorway to our lofty dream suggesting we're not ready to pass through.

Doubt is the quandary that deepens our resolve — the dilemma that fuels imagination and inspires creativity.

Doubt is the robust rivalry between me and you, I and thou — an honorable joust between opposing thoughts and points of view.

Doubt is a tug-of-war between what we will and what we won't — the dubious struggle between resolution and reluctance.

Doubt may well be our truly intuitive tour guide leading us back to circle one, never to be confused with or mistaken for square one; they're entirely different shapes to begin with. Circles, unlike squares, have no straight lines, sharp corners, or properties indicative of confinement.

# CHAPTER 4

---

# Living the Stories
# We Wish to Tell

# Fate and Other Delicious Surprises

Books are given as gifts throughout much of the world, for birthdays, holidays, anniversaries, and the occasional just-because. Those of us who love to read consider our favored books to be great treasures. And when we receive a book as a gift, there's a tendency to treasure it that much more. When we choose a book for someone else — a book we wish to give to another — we never really know how powerful an impact it might have on them or how long its scope of influence might last.

I wasn't much of a reader until I turned fifteen. There were a few books I enjoyed reading before that time, but none that moved me enough to help construct and shape the character that would allow for true alignment with my fate. Up until that time I preferred running, playing, and finding trouble on the streets of old Chicago. I had no deep, undeniable sense of who I was, which isn't unusual at all while we're in the throws of adolescence.

I remember the first book I ever read with a completely open heart and open mind — a book that carried me to and through a realm that could not be forgotten. And how that wonderful little book came to me in the first place is a rather remarkable story in its own right. It was given to me at the age of fifteen by a lovely woman one year shy of twice my age at that time, on a cold, snowy morning in Chicago.

It all began with a glorious feast the night before — food and drink and celebration at one of the finest Greek restaurants ever to exist in the metropolitan Midwest: Diana's — a famous, festive Mediterranean-style restaurant in southwest Chicago.

I was invited to join my sister, her boyfriend, and a friend of theirs I hadn't met before. We arrived at the restaurant and got in line behind thirty or forty people, which was typical and could always be expected at Diana's. And the celebration started right there where you stood. Waiting in line at Diana's was unlike the wait at nearly any other restaurant. Everyone talked, everyone smiled, everyone periodically shouted Opaa! And everyone drank either white or rosé Roditis, provided they were over the age of thirteen. No matter how hungry you felt when you stepped into line, the atmosphere of that well-loved restaurant seemed to pacify even the most starved and impatient patron; after all, it was really the warm, arousing, spectacularly impassioned ambiance we hungered for most. You could taste the metaphors floating through the air, covered with the delightful scents of fresh-cooked food. How many hours of our lives do we spend waiting without any sense of celebration whatsoever? There are things we have to wait for in this world, and it simply makes sense for us to rejoice while we wait, wherever we are and whenever we can, while making the most of the time we've been given.

Finally, after rejoicing in line for nearly an hour, we were seated at a table near the open-hearth fireplace crafted from ancient stones flown in from Athens, we were told. We sat at a round table in the center of the main dining room near enough to that open hearth, which was an extraordinary blessing on wintery nights in the metropolitan Midwest. It was also the ideal spot from which to watch Petros, the gracious, flirtatious, irrepressible host, perform the dance of life while balancing a full glass of wine atop his head, and then for the great, robust, triumphant finale he would drink the wine from the glass he had kept perfectly balanced throughout the dance, then smash the empty glass into the fireplace. "Opaa! Opaa!" we all yelled, as our well-dressed waiter carried our enormous tray of food to our table for four: octopus, leg of lamb, dolmades (grape leaves stuffed with flavorful rice), fried squid, roasted bell peppers, cucumbers with feta cheese and mint leaves, and probably one or two things I've forgotten. And as if all that was not enough, another waiter brought us a seemingly magical flaming cheese held high on route from the kitchen to our table, the soaring fire several feet above our heads adding to the ambiance of myth and magic in an atmosphere of passion and romance.

We ate fine food, drank good wine, and felt the warmth of the fire — on the outside as well as on the inside. We talked openly about those things that mattered most — the things we loved, the things we dreamt about, the things we truly needed. I was the youngest at our table, an eager teen with raging hormones and big dreams. We shared our thoughts and ate great food near the roaring fire, and not once during that lively, joyful, spirited evening did I ever imagine I would wind up spending the remainder of that surprisingly wondrous night with the woman one year shy of twice my age, though that was, in fact, what followed.

She woke me in the morning to let me know she was going out to get us breakfast and to stop at the bookstore across the street to buy a book she said she wanted me to have. She left me alone to reminisce about the sensual fullness of that amazing night of tastefully enlivening celebration. A short time later she returned with warm French toast, pure maple syrup, and a paperback copy of *Siddhartha* by Hermann Hesse, on which she wrote on the inside cover: *Everyone's looking, few people find. I hope that you are one of those who find. Love, Sophia.*

I never saw her again after that day, though what we shared that night and day will be with me forever. The book she chose for me was the ideal gift — the perfect novel for the then young man in search of himself, allowing me to align myself with the pathless path we must pave for ourselves — a path that for me has been paved with poetry and dreams as much as anything. Poetry and dreams — which rise together and come to life while keeping me fully aligned with my destiny. Fate and destiny — those philosophical, fraternal twins with similar traits and distinctly different characteristics; destiny is what we choose to do with the fate we've been given — an empowering distinction that helps keep us on our co-creative paths.

# Determining the Destiny We Question

I remember waking up one morning more than a decade ago — a morning following one of my rare and infrequent dark nights of the soul — only to discover that it was far from over. In fact, it started to look and feel even darker in broad daylight. As the sun rose higher and the air got hotter, I couldn't find my light, joy, warmth, or enthusiasm. Dark nights of the soul seem darker, weightier, and all the more ominous when they greet you on mornings bathed in balmy luminosity while you remain utterly impervious to every bit of splendor flooding forth. And the clouds that tend to follow us around on days like that seem saturated with the questions that must be asked — the questions we must ask ourselves. One of the clouds that followed me that day held the defining question that would shape the course of my life and allow me to honor my destiny.

Fate may be written for us before we can think and breathe freely, but our destinies are largely determined by what we do; by what we choose to devote our lives to.

Back to the question that hovered over my head like a seemingly solid cloud immune to sunshine — an ominous cloud disguised as a question; or was it a question disguised as a cloud? Either way, it was dark, it was heavy, and it needed to be asked and answered that very day, without refrain; because my very life depended on it and that cloud above my head would not go away. The more I looked at it, the more I began to believe that it carried within it a kind of energy akin to a bolt of lightening, capable of killing my true spirit if I were to answer that dangling question incorrectly. The question was: Am I really a writer? Was I or could I ever be a writer of consequence, a writer of substance, a genuine writer who could in fact make a difference? It was the mother of all questions for me at that moment. It was the most significant question I could possibly ask because it was really asking me who I truly was.

And so there I was, facing the question that held the power to determine whether or not I would honor my fate — the question I needed to take hold of and be willing to dance with in order to determine my own true destiny. And how could I dance with a question like that while the music of my heart was still so eerily silent? "Dance anyway," I heard the artist within me continue to say. "Ask anyway, even if you're afraid to get the answer you don't want."

I wanted to join the ranks of the many writers I admired — the wordy immortals who continue touching the hearts and minds of men and women century after century. Did I have what it would take to become one of them? Did I have the skill, passion, and necessary discipline to dig deep enough into the soul of my own humanity to lay the ink-stained tracks of something lasting? And if it turned out that I didn't, could I bear that? Did I have something to say worthy of the road I was seeing before me? It was clearly a do-or-die, moment-of-truth situation, and I had little choice but to bear the weight of it, face the question, and answer it — not only honestly, but also correctly.

Is an honest answer always accurate? Or do we determine what is ultimately true for us by doing what we know we need to do? The gospels of our lives are fundamentally established through the actions we align with our deepest thoughts, infused with all the emotion we need to sustain our greatest visions, goals, and dreams.

I wanted to tell this story in straightforward, no-nonsense, to-the-point fashion; though truth be told, cut-to-the-chase storytelling has never really been my forte. I am, however, fully committed to conveying this story faithfully and accurately all the way to the point at which it ends. It's good to have an ending to point at, but what we discover along the way is always the point.

Let me get back to that notable day and the question that dangled above my head like a large, dark, menacing cloud. I needed to leave my house before the thoughts in that dark gray mass of icy emotion could suck me into the vortex of utter uncertainty that seemed to be getting darker and growing larger every second I sat motionless with my sense of overwhelm. I was beginning to believe that the weight and shear size of it might put cracks in the walls and shatter the windows in my living room.

So where do you go on a dark day of the soul in Southern California, where I lived back then, and still do? I'm not that far from Malibu — from the soft, sandy beaches that line our Pacific shore. Though right outside my own front door there is a fertile landscape filled with oaks, evergreens, birch, mimosa, and plenty of plum trees. And across the road there are flowing hills with ample footpaths that wind through another kind of wilderness. I am totally surrounded by lush hills. A short drive through the canyon leads me to the sandy beaches of

Malibu — two very rich possibilities… though that day I opted for the city instead.

I wanted to hang out with some of the robust spirits of the wordy ones — with some of the writers who seem immortal by virtue of what they managed to lay down. After all, I wanted to be one of them — one of the prolific writers who live for centuries. I wanted to be one of the prodigious poet-philosophers who continue to dance in the hearts and minds of the many generations still to come, and to be known and loved by those who live in this amazing time. I write because I need to write, though somewhere in the front or back or middle of my awareness is the desire to touch, inspire, and lift the hearts and minds of the many.

So I got in my car and drove to the Bodhi Tree Bookstore, a well-known independent establishment in Los Angeles. I was lucky enough to find a safe and legal parking space waiting for me when I got there, a rare find in that bustling part of town. I grabbed my wallet and my keys and made my way to the bookstore, moving as gracefully as one possibly can with the weight of the world resting firmly on one's shoulders.

I made my way to the concrete steps that lead to the creaky door embellished with Tibetan bells that had a hopeful ring as I sauntered in, hoping to find refuge with the spirits who live among the shelves. I stepped gingerly across the wooden floors that lead from aisle to aisle, author to author, shelf to shelf. I wasn't looking for any author in particular, at least not consciously. My eyes were clouded with the question that seemed to be demanding an immediate answer, and I still couldn't find one in the dark, wooden floor my eyes were fixed upon.

Then I looked up... and the one book boldly reaching forward, leaning two to three inches beyond the edge of the shelf, was *Henry Miller on Writing*. Since it reached out to me, I reached back and plucked it from the shelf. Henry Miller had long been one of the writers I admired. Had he been more in touch with his tender, vulnerable, poetic nature, Henry might have been me. I stood in the aisle between M and N, in front of the shelves where Henry Miller and Anais Nin still live together. I stood holding that book I took from the shelf, and then opened it at random to the following passage found on page 19:

> I had to learn, as Balzac did, that one must write volumes before signing one's own name. I had to learn, as I soon did, that one must give up everything and not do anything else but write; that one must write and write and write, even if everybody in the world advises you against it, even if nobody believes in you. Perhaps one does it just because nobody believes; perhaps the real secret lies in making people believe.

I read that passage and knew immediately that my old friend Henry had written it just for me. At least it felt that way as I stood there at that moment. In fact, those words surged through my veins like intravenous anti-venom, saving me from an otherwise lethal snake bite.

The question had been answered. I am a writer as long as I remain fully committed to my willingness to write. And from that day forward to this one, I have never doubted myself the way I did that day. I've had my doubts since then, though not to the point of seriously considering throwing in the literary towel.

# Scent, Snow, and the Ongoing Question

It was the winter of the third year of my life. I'm not entirely certain what month it was, though the snow on the ground and the chill in the air makes me want to guess that it was January. January tends to be a cold and snowy time of year throughout much of the Midwest, which is where I began the odyssey of this life. I was born in the Windy City — Chicago, Illinois — great museums, fabulous food, a famous lakefront, and two of the tallest buildings in the world, neither of which had yet been built at the time this story I'm beginning to tell you took place — a story that may seem small next to a giant skyscraper, but remains meaningful, if not monumental, in my memory.

And so, one snowy day in old Chicago, I visited a bakery with my mother. I remember being carried part of the way, leaning my hood-covered head against the padded shoulder of her woolen coat, moving through that winter world, smiling at the cold that could not touch me. It didn't stand a chance against my coat, hood, mittens, and the warmth of my mother. There's something magical about staying warm in the middle of winter, feeling impervious to icy winds that wield the power to make us shiver if and when we are not dressed appropriately or lack proper love and affection, although the latter produces a deeper and more agonizing chill, without a doubt.

I walked into the bakery on my own, ahead of my mother, mesmerized by the scent of cookies, cakes, breads, and pastries, freshly baked with the fresh scent wafting through crisp, winter air. My mother grabbed a number and got me a cookie, and then we took our place in line and waited for our number to be shouted.

I was in the middle of my third year of life — my fourteenth season outside the womb, a time when strangers were not instantaneously suspect, especially the elders, like the crone my mother spoke to while we waited — the old woman she asked to keep an eye on me while she placed her bakery order. And that haggard old woman wearing heavy, dark clothing was all too willing to oblige.

"Come — stand over here," she said, "away from the glass so people can see what they want." I knew what I didn't want, which was to be standing near the rear wall of a busy bakery with a three-hundred-year-old woman dressed in black. I'm sure she wasn't really as old as all that, but she seemed rather ancient to me at the time. "What's your name?" she asked — a simple question that I was fully prepared to answer.

"My name is Wayne," I told her.

"Wany?" she replied in a questioning tone.

"No. My name is Wayne," I told her once again.

And from that simple, standard question, which I had now answered twice, came the second question — a monumental leap to one of the deepest and most perplexing questions we can ask a child of any age: "What do you want to be when you grow up?"

The instant I heard her ask the question I knew the answer, regardless of my age, innocence, and presumed naivety. I knew at that very moment what I wanted to be. And I didn't hesitate to proudly tell my not-so-grand inquisitor. I stood straight and tall in my approximately three-foot frame, looked directly into the old woman's watery eyes, and told her, "I want to be a lion!"

"A lion," she said, with a look of disapproval and surprise. "You can't be a lion. A lion is an animal. You're a person — a human being. And a human being can't ever be an animal. Do you understand?" she asked.

I nodded my head yes, hoping to quiet her down and make her take a moment to feel my disappointment. It wasn't as if I had worked and planned to become a successful lion my entire life — all three-and-a-half years of it. I simply imagined how amazing it would be to be a lion. I wasn't entirely certain it was not possible at the time, though the crone of a woman who had asked the question made it clear to me that being a lion was out of the question — not an option, hope, prayer, or possibility. I could still see my mother standing at the bakery counter, taking what seemed like an eternity to place her order.

"So, Wany," — she still couldn't say my name correctly — "what do you want to be when you grow up?" This old crone was relentless. She wasn't about to give up the question until I got it right.

So there I was, standing near the rear wall of a very busy bakery, held captive by a relentless old woman armed with a question to which she was determined to get an answer: Wany — Wayne... what do you want to be when you grow up? Now that I had learned and understood the limitations, the laws and physics forever in place, narrowing the options in order to keep us aligned with only the genuine possibilities in regard to what we wish and want to be — now that I knew I could see lions on television and at the zoo but could not become one no matter how much I admired them, I felt pretty confident that I would answer the question correctly from my inquisitor's point of view. I stood straight, gathered my thoughts, looked once again into the eyes of my interrogator, and told her, "I want to be an Indian!" Next to being a lion, which I now knew I could not be, being an Indian seemed to be the next best possible thing. The men got to hunt with bows and arrows, ride horses without their shirts on, roam free, sleep in tipis, and dance around blazing fires with all their friends. That, to me, seemed like a great way to live — lots of fun, excitement, and adventure.

I felt pretty happy about my second choice. My inquisitor, on the other hand, did not look happy at all. She gave me the unmistakable look of disappointment, disapproval, and disbelief all rolled into one. "You can't be an Indian," she said with a bit of a sneer.

"Why can't I be an Indian?" I asked. "Indians aren't animals. An Indian is a person, like you told me I needed to be."

"Because they're not the same kind of people we are," she said. "An Indian is a different kind of person from you. You're white. Indians aren't white... they're red! Do you understand?"

No, I didn't. And not because I was only three years old, but because I knew better. I didn't want to understand that rigid distinction between human beings — the primary pigmentary explanation that separates us from our own humanity. I didn't share my inquisitor's point of view, and I had no wish to. I was three years old, and I knew better. My life experience was limited and I was still free of any formal education and the typically biased filters that tend to come with experience. I was still thinking with the instinct we are taught to abandon and are encouraged to forget for the sake of maturity. Conformity gets mistaken for maturity much of the time.

So... what did I want to do, and thus become, when I grew up? The question of questions, which carries within it the seed of divine potentiality — the energy that moves us from thought to thought and through the actions required to shape the character needed to define the fate that steers us to and through the destiny we undoubtedly co-create. What do you want to "be" when you grow up? is such an immensely complex question for essentially everyone that many choose a path that does not suit or serve them simply to lessen the weight of the question they feel ill-equipped to answer.

I was five years old the first time I heard Elvis sing. And I knew, right then and there, that I wanted to be a singer. When I turned six I felt strongly about becoming a doctor. And at the age of seven I realized that I needed to be a savior. Not *the* savior or the messiah — please let me make that perfectly clear. What I realized at that early age was the need to be the steward of my dreams and the savior of the words that were part of the lexicon I came in with — the language written into my own soul. I felt compelled to tell a true and meaningful story which I had yet to fully live. I wanted to tell a meaningful story — an inspirational, true-life story — and claim it as my own.

Of course, a real-life story can't be claimed until it has been lived sufficiently. And that takes time. It takes courage and necessary struggle. It requires a unique form of faithful openness to live the many moments of your life as fully as possible — the mundane and the miraculous, the ordinary and the exalted, the painful instances you wish to pass through quickly as well as those pivotal moments of bliss you attempt to prolong. You need to live them all as completely as possible in order to sustain the memories you must return to in order to tell your story truthfully. If that is the fundamental task that you've been given — the primary undertaking that determines the destiny held in your hands, you must be the messiah of your own unique understanding in order to tell your story faithfully.

It takes courage to live within the openness of your own life in order to become the flow of all your thoughts, the great cascade of true emotion, and the sacred amalgamation of all your actions. What you choose to do with the life you've been given — that, more than anything, becomes your story. If you think and think, but fail to act, your life becomes a story of collective regret. A full life — a real life, a true life — involves a magical mix of ups and downs and twists and turns that lead you through multiple moments of supposed failure and into your hours of success.

Its seems like an eternity since I stood near the rear wall of that busy bakery, waiting for my mother, attempting to figure out what I wanted to be when I grew up. I have lived through many amazing transformations since that day that have led me to this one; from my desire to be a lion, an Indian, a doctor, and a singer to finally the savior of my own thoughts and dreams. That, of course, is the short list, as opposed to the long list of options and possibilities I considered along the way. There was no way to know the lasting impact of that anything-but-mundane stop along the way. At three years old there was no way to know how long I'd be haunted by the question I was asked that day I visited a neighborhood bakery with my mother, or that all of my collective thoughts and actions that followed after would make me into the writer I've become — the impassioned poet and brother to the baker by virtue of the essential task of nourishing the many hungry souls who share my world, this world, our world.

# On Learning to Ride a Bicycle

It was an early summer day in old Chicago, near the end of June, less than a full week after my fifth birthday the day I decided it was time to learn how to ride a bicycle, a two-wheeler, a "big boy bike"! Clearly I had outgrown my three-wheeled tractor by more than a Windy-City mile. I instinctively knew this would be a learning adventure that required more than mere balance alone, but momentum as well — the joyful momentum of moving as weightlessly as those slow, innocent summer winds that seemed to punctuate my early, eager memories in the making, such as the day I learned how to ride a bicycle.

> *"One of the most important days of my life was when I learned to ride a bicycle."*
> — *Michael Palin*

The moment I saw that dull, red, paint-chipped bicycle, leaning so noticeably against the cold brick wall of the house next door, I knew right then and there what I needed to do. It was waiting there like a lonely, metal, two-wheeled friend, begging to be borrowed for the sake of adventure. I was still young enough to understand the language of inanimate things and still open enough to listen. I knew precisely what it was asking me to do, and I didn't want to risk hurting its feelings by refusing. Nor did I have any wish to. I simply had to seize that less-than-shiny though perfect-sized bike and allow it to teach me how to ride like the wind. And since I was relatively certain that my neighbors weren't home, there was no other choice but to grant myself permission to do what I wanted and needed to do. There was no one around to ask, so I asked myself, and I said YES!

My excitement mounted as I stepped slowly toward the wall my two-wheeled friend was leaning against. Then, taking hold of the handle bars, I wheeled that now officially borrowed (without permission) bicycle onto the sidewalk outside our house. I was all alone. It was the middle of a day near the end of June. Even my imaginary friends were nowhere to be found. There wasn't anyone around to coax or coach me; no one nearby to help me find my balance at such an important start. There were only me and my instincts as to how to begin. My rambunctious nature gave me a bit of an edge, making me daring and determined enough to discover my joyful balance and empowering buoyancy and allowing me sail along the sidewalks of my truly adventurous five-year-old life.

How to begin? That's always the question. How do we ever learn anything new without some degree of eagerness to do so? I was certainly eager enough, although eagerness alone isn't always enough to steady us or guarantee the success of every daring endeavor. There are times, however, when an impulse is the ideal prompt — the perfectly appropriate, spontaneous inspiration guiding us in the direction we ought to go. **An impulse fueled by eagerness has its own equilibrium carried in the hub of pure incentive.** And when that incentive is fully aligned with our own, we find the balance needed to ride like the wind or to center ourselves in the task at hand. My task, that day, was to meet the challenge and master the skill of perpetual motion (via a borrowed bicycle) by pedaling into an exciting new phase of my still so young and innocent life. And I knew I needed to learn quickly — before my neighbors got home to offer me the reminder, the indisputable fact that this old bike did not belong to me!

I knew I needed to make the most of this borrowed bike and the time I granted myself to learn how to ride it. And without further ado or wasteful hesitation, I started running with that bicycle beside me, holding those handlebars with a firm though exuberant grip, then hopping on while both the bike and I were in unified motion. I glided for fifteen to twenty yards before beginning to peddle. I peddled my way round the block twice, without needing, wanting, or even thinking about stopping. Then a third time round to reinforce my newly acquired bicycle skill.

What a thrill it was to glide so effortlessly over the sidewalks of my youth! What a joyful discovery riding a two-wheeler was for me! The sheer exhilaration of self-propelled speed made me understandably giddy. I had taught myself how to ride a big boy bike for heaven's sake, and I was feeling proud, courageous, and unstoppable! I had learned something new by paying attention to that impetuous itch and allowing my instincts to coach me. This was my maiden voyage by way of bike, and I was determined to make the most of it. I remember standing up with my feet placed securely on both peddles and coasting along where the sidewalk sloped downward a little, allowing gravity to give me an invisible boost. And when the sidewalk flattened out again I peddled like a whimsical child eager for speed, turning that old red bike into an imaginary motorcycle.

Movement, speed, grace, momentum… I was decidedly lost in my new *joie de vivre*, in the midst of my fourth rotation round the block, when something occurred to me that I hadn't once thought of, which was "How in the world do I stop?" I had been so swept up in the spontaneous urge to teach myself to ride that I simply followed my impulse without any thought or consideration of the inevitable and eventual need to stop. And just as there was no one around to help me get started, no one had shown up to advise or instruct me about how best to come to a stop.

*"Life is like a bicycle, to keep your balance you must keep moving."*
— *Albert Einstein*

This can seem like a somewhat oversimplified old cliché were it not for the fact that it steers us toward a still relevant truth. Balance and movement — balance through movement… we see it every single day. The world is in perpetual flux, and we do what we do to best keep up with it. We do what we must to keep our balance in this fast-paced, steadily shifting, ever-unfolding, sometimes overwhelming, nonstop, round and round, hurry up, faster-faster, high-speed, out of control, tenaciously senseless acceleration that robs us of our healthy and exquisite equilibrium. Einstein said, with respect to his "Life is like a bicycle" quote, "I thought of that while I was actually riding a bike." So life is like a bicycle when we're actually riding one, and perhaps not quite as much when we aren't. Life is precisely like whatever we're engaged in at the moment. Life is exactly what we're thinking, doing, and being while we're busy being as present as possible. And it simply makes sense for us to enjoy the ride as much and as often as we can.

I realize that I've taken us on a circuitous route to revealing how I came to a stop that day, for reasons rather similar to why I rode around the block as many times as I did: I was enjoying the ride — the freedom, ease, and thrill of acceleration. That and the fact that I hadn't really thought about where and how to come to a stop. In that very same sense, and in much the same way, this is me, both man and boy, riding round this loquacious neighborhood looking for the perfect place to stop.

How we do anything is how we do everything, the Zen proverb tells us. It's been fifty-plus years since I first seized the time, borrowed a bike, and taught myself how to ride it. More than five full decades have miraculously passed between that noteworthy day and this one. And I keep leaping onto the page with a bit of a running start, much as I leapt onto that borrowed bike with the determination to ride it. I keep leaping onto the page while my life is in motion, gliding like an obstreperous child over the proverbial sidewalks of my second youth. The first was the one I intermittently played and struggled on during my actual childhood days. The second is the one I intermittently play and struggle on now in the midst of my many written recreations.

Our struggles — both joyful and otherwise — allow us to shape our characters and construct our lives in ways that wouldn't be possible without them. They permit us to temper our spirits, set our goals, streamline our intentions, and strengthen our resolves to see them through. Our honest struggles are not in the way, but are the way through a fully lived life.

The way we do anything is the way we do everything, to paraphrase that insightful proverb. The longer I live and the younger I become, the more I value my deepening understanding of that potent little proverb.

Now that I've written the equivalent of five rotations round the block, and my bicycle story seems to be winding down, I need to tell you how I finally came to a stop. I relied on impulse and intuition at the start, in the absence of any reassuring words or steadying hand from my mom, dad, or trustworthy guardian. And once again it was simply me and my instincts as to how to slow myself down and come to a comparatively safe and graceful stop.

First I removed my sneaker-clad feet from those well-worn rubber peddles, permitting gravity to reduce my speed and slow my momentum. And once I slowed to the point at which balance became a bit more challenging, I spotted a soft, green, glistening patch of freshly cut grass and spontaneously rolled myself onto it. I considered it the perfect way to end such a memorable ride — a delightful first ride followed by a joyful roll. And neither I nor the bike I borrowed was the least bit injured. No bruises or grass stains to be worn as my badge of courage, which would have required an explanation to my parents in the aftermath of my unaccompanied victory. And yet it was a victory, even though I was the only one there to actually witness it. It felt like a victory as I looked up at the world from the grassy landscape I had landed on. I felt a little bigger, a little older, and better equipped to ride through the ups and downs of my five-year-old life. I stood up proudly, picked up that bike, walked my two-wheeled friend and mentor back to where I had found it, leaned it securely against the wall, and glided home with my joyful sense of triumph. I walked back home feeling like a bigger and somehow better boy by virtue of my solitary conquest.

# The Wisdom of Innocence

I wanted to steal back innocence and carry it into the forefront; snatch it from the credulous depths of coerced obscurity; hoist it up, dust it off, and give it a proper name. I wanted to take a tiny step forward — and back — to a time when I knew that I was art and artist, creation and creator, spontaneity and destiny, inextricably woven into the universal womb of endless wonder. I could tell you that pen-and-paper has been my savior, my teacher, my friend in need. I could confess the very same thing to myself, even though I already know it to be true. That being said, I have no objection to telling myself what I already know, since there are so many styles, levels, and degrees of knowing what we know.

I wanted to bring innocence into the center again, walk it back from the illusory outskirts of an arid and infertile oblivion, and simply listen to whatever it needed to say…

Once upon a time I was a child fueled largely by curiosity and its imaginative twin. Before I entered the womb, I was a whisper. And before that whisper was heard, I was merely the essence of an incandescent dragonfly hovering over a lake I would later come to know as the lake of my youth. Before that I was the sunlight permitting those phosphorescent dragonfly wings to glisten in the radiance of wonder. And before that… chances are I was the stone I'm now holding in my hand.

We can think back and back *ad infinitum* and never come close to a finite beginning. "So why not start with innocence," I keep asking myself. And sometimes I have sense enough to listen. These, then, are simply the whimsical scribbles of ongoing innocence — rising from the cobalt-blue ashes of a fiery dream; or the aftermath of an inkwell eruption leaving serendipitous word stains on the luminous walls of my psyche.

Maturity is what we trick ourselves into. Innocence, on the other hand, is where our passions to live full and astonishing lives reside. Innocence offers us the bountiful and benevolent plentitude we use to shape and build the free and wild fullness of our lives. The land of eternal youth awaits those who learn to honor and act accordingly from the spirit of innocence.

All we can do is pour our hearts out every day, knowing that life (our lives) depends on the fullness of our giving. All we can do is give it all — every precious, potent, bloody drop of our crazy, delicious, creative madness, knowing we can never give enough — and when we're empty; fatigued; nearly done in by our impassioned battle to be better than we were the day, year, or decade before, take one full breath and let everything go… collapse into the parabolic lap of the ecstatic, surrendering to the only dreams that allow and encourage us to continue. The breath remembers what the mind forgets.

# ABOUT THE AUTHOR

Wayne Allen LeVine is writer, poet, philosopher, storyteller, impassioned public speaker and author. LeVine's previously published books include *Forgiveness for Forgotten Dreams, Myths & Artists*, the Amazon.com Best Seller *Insights of an Ordinary Man*, and now his long awaited *THE FOURTH REFLECTION* has arrived! Wayne Allen LeVine's poems and stories have been included in several award-winning journals and on-line magazines, such as *Rattle, the Examiner.com*, and several editions of the Best-Selling *Chicken Soup for the Soul series*, including *Chicken Soup for the Body and Soul*. A Midwestern son -- born and raised in The Windy City, currently resides in Southern California with his wife and their two rock star sons.